Great Ideas for
Kids' Rooms

Great Ideas for
Kids' Rooms

Bath · ew York · Singapore · Hong Kong · Co ogne · De hi · Melbourne

This is a Parragon Publishing Book

Copyright © Parragon Books Ltd

Parragon Books Ltd
Queen Street House
4 Queen Street
Bath BA1 1HE, UK

Original text: Cristian Campos
Art direction: Mireia Casanovas Soley
Layout: Emma Termes Parera

Copyright © 2009 Parragon Books for the English edition

English edition produced by: APE International, Richmond, VA
Translation: Mary Dobrian, Cologne. for APE International

ISBN 978-1-4075-5274-3

Printed in China

Introduction

Decorating a child's room in a creative way calls for imagination and flexibility. Little people often grow much faster than their parents would like them to—and naturally, their interests and preferences change just as quickly. For you as a parent, it is not always easy to keep up with these changes. After all, you want your child to feel happy and at home in his or her room and to enjoy spending time there.

When your child becomes a teenager, at the very latest, your creativity will really be put to the test. At that age, play space takes on secondary importance. Teenagers want to have a little world of their own, where their privacy and individuality are taken seriously—but where they can still do their homework.

Many of the designers and interior decorators who design and furnish children's rooms actually know very little about children's developmental stages. On the other hand, many educators have a similar lack of knowledge when it comes to furnishing children's rooms in a practical manner that will also satisfy the wishes of their young inhabitants. In this book, we aim to bridge those gaps and provide all parents with good—and above all, realistic—hands-on tips for designing creative children's rooms.

It is not uncommon that interior decorators who are given the task of designing a child's room will neglect to consult with their actual client. They will frequently ask the parents what they envision for the design, but not the child who is going to live in the room. However, as parents you can very easily learn from your children what they like and what they would like to change.

People like to talk about the "secret language" of children. It is quite possible that it really exists. But children's language is actually not all that mysterious. Insightful parents who know their children well can understand them quite well. All parents feel that their child is unique. Nevertheless, depending on the child's age and personality, there are many common needs and interests that differ only slightly from one child to the next.

Despite the extensive supply of literature on the subject, designing a really great children's room is much simpler and more intuitive than most people think. Just let your imagination go! First and foremost,

what your child needs is a peaceful, friendly, and stimulating environment—not the dry, matter-of-fact office of a university professor. Without a minimum of empathy for your little "customer," you won't be successful.

We are all familiar with those impressive, highly educational designer playgrounds that have been showered with prizes—and where, unfortunately, most child never want to play. Maybe that was the intention to begin with . . . That way, at least, the prizes could be awarded on site without the noise of happily playing children disturbing the ceremony. Here, however, we will only present suggestions for children's rooms in which kids can tumble and play to their hearts' content.

This book will provide you with lots of useful information about your child's different developmental phases. In addition, the effects that these various phases have on children's space requirements and

related needs will be explained. Ask your children what they would like their rooms to look like! Spend some time playfully brainstorming with them about the design of their future little kingdoms.

The chapters in this book focus on the progressive phases of children's growth and development: toddlers, preschool children, elementary school kids, and older children/teenagers. In the appendix, you will also find a small collection of useful suggestions. Most importantly, decorating and furnishing a child's room should be fun for adults and children alike. Nevertheless, it is very important not to lose sight of the educational aspect of the design. This, of course, is primarily the job of the parents.

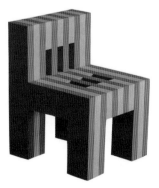

Babies and Toddlers: 0–2 Years

Babies and Toddlers: 0–2 Years

Babies

Small babies don't need much aside from their parents' love and care. Naturally, nearly all parents fall prey to the temptation to furnish their baby's room with much more than just a little crib. Such young children, however, take hardly any interest at all in the furniture in their rooms, to say nothing of the decoration. The only interesting things to them are the bed, the playpen, and the rug or carpet. But since the baby will come in contact with all sorts of objects—such as toys, stuffed animals, blankets, and pillows—it is important to choose these things very carefully.

In the first twelve months of life, a baby develops at lightening speed, both mentally and physically. In the first twelve weeks, newborns experience their environment primarily through sight. During this period they can focus particularly well on large objects. Just a short time later, the baby will already begin curiously touching every object she can get her hands on—and putting it in her mouth as well. At the age of one year your baby will likely already be able to crawl, and sometimes even walk. Now, at the very latest, you should make sure that all breakable objects are out of your little darling's reach before she can put them to their last use ever. A happy baby, surrounded by the wreckage of her toys, is not an unusual sight.

Actually, a crib is the only really necessary item in terms of basic furnishings for a baby's room. Nevertheless, we are usually quite willing to fill up the space with dressers, shelves, a changing table, and a chest or similar container for the many toys.

Here, you basically have two options. Either you can go shopping for new furniture every time your child enters another stage of development, or you can from the beginning buy furniture that "grows" with your child. The latter may be somewhat more expensive at the outset, but it will definitely pay off in the long run. For example, there are cradles or cribs that can be converted into beds for small children. There are height-adjustable chairs and portable changing tables that can later be transformed into dressers. Shelves and chests of drawers do not change much in size as your child grows. But do you think your teenager will still want a dresser decorated with baby motifs? It's best to buy children's furniture that is easy to convert, expand, or rearrange as time goes by.

When purchasing furniture, pay special attention to those pieces that your baby will use for a longer period of time, such as the bed, for example. The bars of a crib should not be more than 2½ inches apart. It is very important that children's furniture does not have any sharp corners or parts that protrude or come off easily. Naturally, it also needs to be stable and very durable. Good furniture stores should be able to provide you with information about safety requirements for children's furniture, and a qualified salesperson will be happy to advise you. Whenever possible, select furniture with rounded corners. Whether or not the furniture matches the rest of your decor is of secondary importance. What matters is that it meets the needs of small children. After all, your child will bump his head against these solid obstacles much more frequently than he is likely to meditate on your design concept.

Take plenty of time to think about what furniture you choose. The pieces should last for several years, even if your child's needs change

somewhat in the meantime. Careful planning from the beginning will save a lot of money and effort in the long run. An impulsive furniture purchase rarely turns out to have been a good decision. Young parents, in particular, frequently make the mistake of outfitting their baby's room with the most modern and trendy accessories without really having an idea of what babies actually need. Yet you don't have to look far to find all the information you require. There are numerous magazines, for example, in which you can find tried and tested advice on furnishing children's rooms. It can even be helpful to leaf through mail-order catalogs. And of course, you can consult with friends who already have experience in this area.

Naturally, a small child's room should be aesthetically appealing, but first and foremost, it needs to be functional. As mentioned earlier, up until a certain age, small children are not terribly interested in the appearance of their rooms anyway. For the first year of life, it is most important that the child's room is comfortable and practical.

 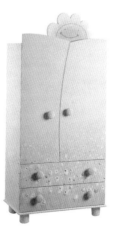 

Nevertheless, the use of color is quite important. Bright, primary colors and strong contrasts help to stimulate a baby's sense of sight—and besides, babies and toddlers simply like them.

We realize that simply painting a wall pink will not transform a hyperactive child's room into an oasis of calm. It is an undeniable fact, however, that colors can impart a basic atmosphere. Pink and blue, for instance, are said to be quiet, calming colors. Green is the color of nature, and yellow is associated with happiness. Some educators believe that small children who live in completely yellow-painted rooms cry more often than others. But whether or not you believe in the psychology of colors, it is better to avoid overly dark tones in very young children's rooms. Little ones usually don't like them, and they swallow up a great deal of light.

When it is time to start making concrete plans, the first thing to do is take exact measurements of the room. Draw a plan that includes the height and position of features such as electrical outlets, windows,

doors, and any built-in closets. Next, you can draw in the furniture you intend to use to furnish the child's room. There are very simple-to-use computer programs that can help you construct this type of plan, if you are so inclined. This helps you avoid a situation in which a furniture purchase turns into a fiasco because your "eyeball" measurement wasn't quite right. Most furniture stores can provide you with a ruler or tape measure if you are unsure about the dimensions of a particular piece.

It's better not to use wallpaper in a small child's room. Removing it later is quite a difficult job, and besides, wallpaper is a magnet for dust—not on the visible side, but rather on the side that is glued to the wall. A better option is to paint the walls with latex paint. This is available in myriad colors and is especially easy to clean. In addition, latex paint dries very quickly and the odor disappears in just a few days. Nevertheless, be sure to paint the room well ahead of time so that the paint is thoroughly dry by the time the little inhabitant

moves in. The odor is not harmful, but it can trigger nausea or other temporary discomforts, and can be particularly bothersome to children with allergies.

Price should not be your first criterion when selecting furniture. While the most expensive pieces are not necessarily the best, good quality does come at a certain price. Don't be seduced by current trends and end up spending too much money just to have a fashionable piece of furniture. Keep in mind that the lifespan of your children's furniture will be quite a bit shorter than that of your living room sofa. Ideally, you should aim to find a good balance between quality, flexibility, and price.

In the first months of life, babies take in their surroundings primarily through the senses of touch and sight—although they can also recognize many different sounds. Thus, they can certainly identify and differentiate between basic moods such as joy, sadness, anger or rejection. Any moving object in their environment will capture

their attention—especially if the object also produces interesting sounds or music.

New parents usually can't imagine how fast children actually grow. There are no rules about how to decorate a child's room—just let your imagination go! Nevertheless, you should keep in mind that extremely baby-oriented accessories will be outgrown in a very short time. It's therefore best to concentrate on the basics—that is, a crib, a playpen, and a dresser or wardrobe—when you first start out furnishing a baby's room. Bedding, toys, and other items play a secondary role. After all, it is much simpler to exchange a curtain, a bedcover, or a pillow than it is to get a whole new bed or dresser.

One problem with overly trendy furniture is that we often feel like replacing it after a relatively short time because we have gotten tired of looking at it. In addition, very fashionable pieces are frequently not very well made. Therefore, some interior designers recommend

buying children's furniture well ahead of time and allowing it to "air" for a few weeks before placing it in the child's room. Logically, this is especially important in the case of furniture made of plastic or compressed wood. This way, you can avoid a situation in which the material releases microscopic particles that may aggravate asthma or other respiratory problems, or even provoke their onset. Best of all, of course, is to buy furniture made of solid wood or other natural materials that do not release any particulate matter into the air at all.

Standard wall-to-wall carpeting is not a good idea for young children's rooms. Over time, it can collect dust and mites—not to mention the crumbs and bits of food that little ones tend to leave everywhere—which can become quite unhygienic. Children who are prone to allergies or asthma can be particularly sensitive to such

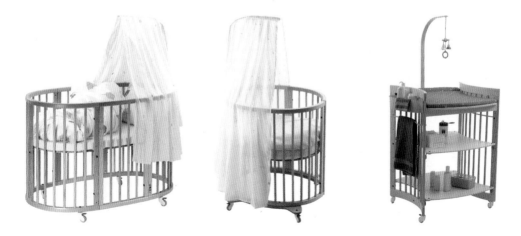

situations. A better alternative is a smooth floor surface such as laminate, parquet, tile, or stone. Small children do love play rugs or blankets and large pillows; just be sure that these items (or their covers) are small enough to fit into a washing machine. You won't be able to get very far against ground-in dirt on a play rug using just a vacuum cleaner. If you do decide to put carpeting in your child's room, you should definitely choose carpet tiles. That makes it easy to exchange individual squares if they become too heavily soiled. Some very high quality carpet tiles are even machine-washable. But no matter which material you choose, make sure that it does not contain any harmful substances. A specialized dealer will be able to provide you with all the necessary information on this subject.

Avoid using wallpaper. It is difficult to remove and is a real dust magnet—particularly on the side that is glued to the wall.

Don't choose the cheapest furniture available. The most expensive pieces are not necessarily the best, but good quality does have its price.

Carefully measure the furniture you select for your baby's room. The bars of a crib should not be more than 2½ inches apart.

Standard carpeting collects mites and dust which can aggravate allergies and asthma. Laminate, parquet, tile, or stone are better floor covering choices.

1-Year-Olds

The second year of a child's life is the phase in which the greatest changes take place. By their sixteenth month, most children can stand and walk on their own. Now they can explore their environment quite independently—and of course, they will encounter a wide variety of obstacles along the way. Your child will now begin trying to dress and undress himself without help, and he will experiment enthusiastically with every object within his reach. Now it is time to make sure that the rest of your home is childproof as well. Furthermore, parents now have to constantly monitor the home—and especially the child's room—and remove every object their child might consider edible (and this means anything he can put into his mouth!) Any furniture that could get in the way of the child's still uncontrolled movements (and unfortunately, this means most of the furniture in any given room), will need to be moved. If you have breakable objects that you value highly, you should move them to a safe place immediately. Sometimes it is simpler to just pack the breakable items away until this particular phase comes to an end. And it will come to an end—even if it is sometimes hard to believe.

At this age, children don't talk very much yet, but they can already understand what people say to them. Even if they don't recognize

particular words, they can certainly interpret the tone in which they are spoken to. Twelve-month-olds can already recognize feelings such as jealousy, fear, anger, affection, etc. For parents, this means that interactions with their children become more complex. As far as this book is concerned, it means that no matter how we arrange and organize our children's rooms, they will adjust them to suit their needs and wishes at any given moment. Toddlers will touch any object within their reach, throw it down, put it in their mouths, and chew on it (in this order). On the other hand, at this age children begin to occupy themselves more and more—meaning that you don't constantly have to entertain them. If you are lucky, after your baby bumps his head for the second time, he will realize that he can't run through a wall head first. Since he will spend a large part of each day pulling himself up on the nearest support, you should concentrate on heavy, solid, and stable furniture. Any unsteady object can now pose a danger, and every loose cable or string—telephone wires, for example—can become a serious tripping hazard for your child.

Wherever possible, hide wires and cables in special boxes or behind molding strips, or simply use wireless appliances.

Between the ages of 14 and 18 months, the little artist in your child will come to life. Now there is no wall, closet, or other potential drawing surface that is safe from your little one's creative impulses. During this "scribble phase," many children also devote a lot of their attention to tearing down wallpaper. Anyone who has ever renovated an apartment can relate to the satisfaction of stripping an entire wall bare, beginning with just one square inch of poorly glued wallpaper. Therefore, if your child's room is wallpapered, it is better not to place her crib directly against the wall.

Another brief word about colors: children love them! Consider painting your child's room in a cheerful combination of bold colors such as yellow, red, green, or blue. It will be much more interesting and fun than boring white or a depressing black or gray.

Go ahead and use bright colors: red, green, blue, etc. Any combination of these colors is also very cheerful.

Every piece of furniture will be an important support for your child's first steps. Therefore, they should stand firmly in place and not tip over under a heavy burden.

If your toddler's crib stands directly beside a papered wall, he might try his hand at mural painting at an early age—or tear off the wallpaper little by little.

2-Year-Olds

A period of enormous physical activity begins around the age of two years. This is the phase of somersaults and attempts to climb up onto any available object. Now your child will delight in any type of plaything that contributes to this newfound mobility. Unfortunately, however, this irresistible urge to move is not without its dangers. It is a good idea to keep a close eye on your toddler during this stage. Set up a play area where he will be visible to you most of the time—maybe in the living room or the kitchen. There are many wonderful play and activity rugs available for this purpose. Your child will also love any kind of little tent (it can even be a large cardboard box) where he can play another of this age group's favorite games: hiding.

Naturally, a two-year-old child is capable of entertaining herself for longer periods of time than a younger baby. After all, she is slowly but surely beginning to learn a few important social rules. One of the most important of these is that she cannot demand other people's attention—not even that of her parents—every moment of the day. Now is the time to buy your child her own little table and chair where she can occupy herself for short periods of time. They should be sturdy but still lightweight enough to be transported from one area of the home to another.

High chairs for feeding toddlers are best placed a short distance away from the wall—or place the chair with its back to the wall if you don't mind having the wall redecorated. A small child who is just learning to feed himself is approximately as active as an uncovered blender, spraying its contents all over the surrounding area.

At the age of two, many children can already speak relatively well, although they still make a lot of mistakes. Now they love having someone read stories or sing songs to them. If you keep picture books within easy reach in a toy box or on shelves, your little listener can choose her book for herself. Be prepared to read the same story many times over!

One piece of furniture that was not important to your child before now becomes especially interesting: the sofa. Toddlers love to climb up on it, hop up and down on it, jump off of the armrests—and occasionally they simply sit down on it, although not usually for very long. Children find the sofa especially fun if you lay a pile of

different-sized pillows on it. These make a great landing place to fall into, and they are also excellent for throwing around. Blankets are also popular at this stage of life. Children can roll around on them, hide underneath them, or just wrap themselves up in them. It is advisable to make sure that the blankets are easily washable, that they do not attract too much dust, and don't pill excessively. And blankets should definitely be as durable as possible. Of course, house pets such as dogs or cats should have their own blankets, which should not come into contact with those of the children.

To sum up, a two-year-old child is beginning to speak and to follow everything that happens around him with the greatest curiosity. His range of activity is no longer limited to his own room; he is now beginning to gradually conquer the entire home. Be sure that there are no heavy objects within your child's reach that could fall down and injure him. You should provide your child with a pleasant play area with an appropriate floor surface. In addition, he needs to have

a place where he can be quiet and rest. If you have stairs in your house or apartment, it is essential to install a small gate at the top and at the bottom to keep your little one from attempting any reckless adventures. These stairway gates are widely available in specialty stores. Of course, your children's toys should always be kept where he can reach them easily.

You can now begin to teach your child that different areas of the home serve different functions. In the beginning, of course, children look at the entire house as one gigantic playground. Over time, however, they learns that their own room, in particular, is a place for sleeping and playing.

Of course, toddlers can also play in the living room or the dining room, especially when their parents are nearby. The kitchen and the bathroom, on the other hand, are not very well suited for playing. At the age of two, children can begin to understand these concepts.

Nevertheless, you should not always shoo your child into her own room to play. Children want to stay in contact with their environment, and at the same time, of course, with you. To begin with, it is fully sufficient to make clear, for example, that your toddler can't play soccer in the kitchen while you are preparing lunch.

Walls painted in light, friendly colors will have a soothing effect on your toddler.

Picture books can be stored in a toy chest or closet, or on shelves.

At this stage, when children have a constant urge to tumble and climb, you should buy furniture that allows them to really romp around. Even a simple play blanket can provide lots of fun for your little one.

Two-year-olds can sit still for short periods of time. They will be delighted with a sturdy yet lightweight chair in their very own size.

Preschool Children: 3–5 Years

Preschool Children: 3–5 Years

Children have their own specific needs, and their rooms should be furnished with just as much care as those of adults. Think for a moment of all the factors to consider when looking for a new apartment to rent or purchase: Is it bright and well located? What kind of a view does it have? Is it easy to keep warm? Will I be able to work here undisturbed? Can I have pleasant gatherings with my friends here? Are there recreation areas nearby? Is the apartment large enough to suit my needs? Before making a decision, we usually weigh these and other, largely subconscious criteria that affect the quality of the apartment. A child will judge the quality of his or her room just as critically: Is it easily accessible? Is the atmosphere warm and comforting or cold and unwelcoming? Do I like the color of the walls? Are the surfaces well padded so I can tumble and play without hurting myself? Do I have enough space?

There are countless colors, shapes, and materials with which children can entertain themselves for hours on end. Most children's furniture—as well as rooms designed especially for children—takes advantage of only a fraction of the possibilities. All of your child's senses come to life during the preschool years. Impressions from the outside world are now becoming more and more important, and he

is learning new things all the time. Many psychological studies have shown that the design of a child's room has an enormous influence on his intellectual development. It should come as no surprise that cramped, dark rooms are less appropriate for children than open, light spaces. Children love to hide and play in small corners where their parents can't see them—but nevertheless, who wants to live in a tiny, dimly lit room?

It's also important to remember that most city children only occasionally have the opportunity to come into direct contact with nature. A person who grows up in a world of stone and glass often knows nothing about how the cows live who produce the milk they drink every day, or that there are many, many more trees and plants in the world than those that grow in boxes on their balcony or in pots in the apartment. Give your child as many opportunities as possible to experience nature directly. House pets such as dogs or cats, of course, are very helpful in this regard. It is a wonderful

experience for a child to grow up with an animal. And if the animal is also a young one, child and pet will get to know each other especially easily and will quickly become inseparable. On the other hand, if the animal was already living in the house before the child is born, jealousies can occasionally develop. With a great sensitivity and consistent training, you can help your four-legged friend understand that the new little person does not intend to take its place. Likewise, your child will need to learn from the very beginning how to behave with an animal.

Preschool-aged children often accumulate a series of ritual activities. As soon as a little person masters a particular skill for the first time and receives praise for it, she will enthusiastically repeat the same activity a dozen times a day. This is completely normal, and a sign of your child's growing self-confidence. This is also the reason that children at this age love to look at the same books and watch the same television programs over and over again. Films and television

series produced for adults are not appropriate for such young children, and they are not even capable of understanding them. There are many lovely and well-produced children's films and series that preschoolers can easily understand. It is only logical, then, that they will want to repeat this satisfying experience over and over. Almost all parents of preschool children have had the experience of reading their child the same book every single day for weeks, or being asked to play the same songs until the whole family knows them by heart. Children simply love to share their experiences with the people who are most important to them. And that means you, dear parents!

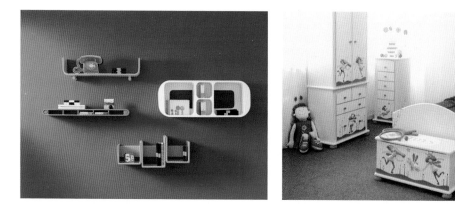

When your child reaches preschool age, you can begin placing objects on shelves again without fear that everything will be knocked over and broken.

Let the sun shine into your child's room whenever possible. But do use curtains or shades to avoid being blinded by the sun.

Colorful boxes are excellent for storing toys and secret treasures.

Now your child can sleep in a real, full-sized bed. Adjustable-length bed frames are particularly practical.

3-Year-Olds

At the age of about three years, children begin to live more and more according to the social rules of the adult world, and in doing so to display a certain degree of maturity. Now your child learns to tell the difference between truths and lies, and gradually begins to distinguish between reality and fantasy. On the whole, three-year-olds communicate much more intensely with both their parents and their environment. A typical characteristic of this age group is an alternation between great self-assurance (through which every "no" ends in a temper tantrum) and sudden insecurity and vulnerability. The most important change, however, is your child's growing self-confidence. He becomes more and more independent and suddenly wants to do everything all by himself—particularly day-to-day tasks. In this way, he can demonstrate his skill and intelligence both to himself and to those around him.

As far as everyday life is concerned, this means that children will now begin to make use of the entire apartment to a much greater extent. In the course of their play, they alternate between peak athletic performance and longer periods of quiet activity. They draw, listen to stories, build with blocks, or examine everyday objects. In the course of these activities, they often sit at tables that are either

much too large or much too small for them. Be sure to provide your child with an appropriately sized table at which she can work and play. Tables that "grow with" your child are especially practical and are often available with corresponding chairs. This type of furniture may not be inexpensive, but it is definitely a worthwhile investment. Nevertheless, some children will still prefer to sit on a sofa or a few pillows, depending on the activity.

A child's bed should be placed in such a way that he always has a good view of the door and doesn't need to turn his head when someone comes into the room. This will help him feel more secure and will usually help him sleep more peacefully.

Another room of the house that will now become part of your child's world is the bathroom. Since bathroom fixtures are tightly secured in place, the room can only be adapted to your child's size to a limited degree. Fortunately, most of your problems can be easily solved with the help of small accessories, such as a stepstool in front of the sink.

Just like adults, children will not want to wash themselves in a cold or smelly bathroom, so be sure that the room is sufficiently heated and ventilated. Particularly in winter, warm towels are a great hit with children. Compared to other rooms in the house, the atmosphere of a bathroom can often seem "cold" to youngsters. You can counteract this impression with touches such as a cheerful, colorful bathmat. If you decorate your bathroom in an inviting style and always keep it warm, your child is less likely to develop an aversion to taking a shower or bath.

Participation in group games is another important new development during this period. Up to now, your child has primarily played either alone or with you. Actually, she only needed to have someone there to do the things she couldn't do herself, such as turning the pages of a book, handing her a puppet—or picking it up again after she threw it across the room. She could devote an astonishing amount of time and patient attention to watching a piece of paper swirl and flutter

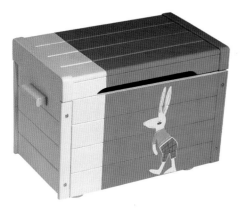

to the ground. But at the age of three, this kind of play gradually becomes boring for children. More and more often, your little one will want to do things together with other people. Now is the time to introduce the first games with learning value. Such games can foster a variety of skills, the most important of which are intellectual and physical flexibility. At the same time, social games teach children about interacting with others. Games can be good practice for a variety of social rules, which are becoming more and more important at this age. For example, your child can learn that certain behavior that was tolerated when she was younger is no longer acceptable, and that she needs to take more responsibility for herself and her possessions. At this age, most children's motor skills are so well developed that they can turn the pages of a book by themselves and handle their toys with more care.

As children grow older, the number of toys they own typically increases as well. But where to put them all? Of course, children

would like to be able to see all their toys at the same time, so shelves and open boxes are ideal at this stage. However, you can also introduce your child to the idea of a "treasure chest" where she can hide her most important items. Most children find this very exciting and can quickly learn that each object has its own particular place. You can decorate a chest together with your child using paints or stickers—perhaps with an ocean or pirate motif—making it all the more interesting for your child. Nevertheless, a few toys should always be available for the next day's play—preferably in a place where no one will trip over them. Don't even try to establish a perfect system of order in your child's room; you will just end up frustrating yourself. Still, you can make it clear to your child that the toys she scatters throughout the apartment during the day need to be returned to her own room every evening. This way, she can quickly learn to distinguish between her own room and the spaces that are used by all the members of the family.

When selecting the most suitable material for children's furniture or toys, wood is always an optimal choice. Most children like it a lot as well. Plastic is certainly attractive because of its many bright colors; however, it often contains harmful materials and it is not nearly as durable as wood. In addition, at this age, children are not capable of identifying plastic as an artificial material and will tend to assume that it is something natural. Wood, on the other hand, is more durable and conveys much more warmth. You can easily associate it with nature in your child's mind simply by pointing to a tree outside the door. Many wooden blocks are available in brilliant signal colors, but it is also nice to buy a few wooden toys in their natural state and paint them together with your child. You will see that he will throw himself into the task enthusiastically—and at the same time, he can begin to learn how two colors can be mixed together to produce a third.

When furnishing a child's room, you should always keep in mind that children and adults simply don't share the same tastes. For example, a child will find a potted plant much more attractive than a vase of flowers, because it reminds her of nature and of how much fun it is to play in the forest or the park. Furthermore, vases are more easily knocked over and broken. When small children are just learning to stand up and walk, however, tall plants or potted trees placed within their reach are not a good idea, since the little ones will invariably try to use the plant as a support. For you, this means that in addition to the danger of injury from a falling plant, you will have to clean spilled potting soil off the floor, perhaps on a daily basis.

Children like bold symbols that they can understand easily. For child-friendly interior decorating, it is best to use very simple imagery. Together with your child, you can design and paint simple, colorful pictograms for routine activities such as bedtime, supper time, brushing teeth, etc. You can then hang these pictures up in the appropriate

locations throughout the house or apartment. This is a simple and entertaining way to teach your child about the activities that take place in each particular area of the home. Children love variation in the organization of their daily routine. By the way, this approach also works well for adults who want to practice a foreign language. Simply attach small slips of paper containing vocabulary words to the corresponding objects, e.g. lamp, computer, radiator, etc.

Preschool-aged children love little windows or openings that connect two rooms to each other—the kitchen and the dining room, for example. But you don't need to break a hole through a wall if you don't already have one: some toy manufacturers offer relatively large square or rectangular building components made of especially lightweight material. Children can use such pieces to restructure their own spaces with little windows, nooks, and crannies.

A chalkboard is a wonderful addition to a child's room. It constantly provides new impulses for creativity.

Pictures containing simple images make particularly good wall decorations for children. You can draw or paint some together with your child.

Ideally, your child's bed should be placed so that she can see the doorway of her room any time, without having to turn her head. This will give her a feeling of safety and calm.

A children's table and appropriately-sized chairs will help prevent poor posture.

4-Year-Olds

A child's personality really begins to emerge around the age of four. For many of us, our earliest childhood memories can also be traced back to this period. Four-year-olds want to spend more and more time with other people and to play together with others. In this way, preschoolers learn about social behavior norms as well as conflicts with others. Many children learn to dress and undress themselves at this age. They constantly want to try new things and expand their range of possibilities: they want to ride a bike unassisted, learn to swim or play soccer. This is also the age at which they begin to compare all sorts of abilities with those of other children. And they enthusiastically bombard their parents with questions in their constant thirst for more information: why, why, why?

It is an ideal situation if a child's room can grow along with its young inhabitant. If your child is old enough to get dressed on his own, he will also want to choose the clothing himself. Keep in mind that he is growing very quickly, and a wardrobe or dresser that was once the right size will soon be too low. A good alternative to traditional wardrobes are boxes on wheels that let you store the clothes under the bed. Rolling the box out from under the bed, picking out his things, and then letting it disappear again will also be fun for your child.

Many children now have the desire to transform their rooms more and more into a "safe place." This is a sign of their growing independence. Furthermore, in the security of her own little kingdom, your child can protect her toys and other treasures from the grasp of other children and members of the household (including the adults). At this age, most children still don't like to share their possessions with others.

Colorful crates and boxes are excellent for storing toys. Your child's things should be spread throughout the room only when he is really using them. A four-year-old is already old enough to pick up his own toys when he is finished playing with them. Nevertheless, you should be content when your child simply stuffs everything into a box; it doesn't have to be well organized. Children at this age love to make a mess of everything they get their hands on, anyway. Up until now, your child may have frequently reduced his dolls, stuffed animals, and every other type of toy to their individual pieces. This probably

doesn't happen so often anymore, but nevertheless, you will find the pieces spread throughout the entire apartment.

It takes strong nerves to constantly tell your child to put her things away—and it usually doesn't work very well, anyway. Now, at the latest, is the time to provide your child with a large toy box or "treasure chest" into which all of her toys will fit. This will save you the tedious process of sorting everything onto shelves, into cupboards, or into lots of little boxes. This kind of order is not really important to a preschool child, and chances are that she will enthusiastically pull everything out again and throw it on the floor. Decorating the toy box together with your child, according to her taste, will make picking up all the more fun.

For preschool children, the furniture in their rooms not only serves a practical function; they also enjoy playing with it. Therefore, very massive or difficult-to-move pieces are not especially popular with

small children. On the other hand, furniture that is too lightweight could fall over during play and possibly even injure your child. Pieces made of lightweight wood are a good choice that strikes a balance between these extremes.

Did you just buy a new television set? Whatever you do, don't throw away the big cardboard box that it came in! It can provide your child with countless hours of fun. What looks like just a big box to you can be a racecar, a robber's cave, or all kinds of other things to him. Pay attention to which toys your child likes to play with best. This will give you lots of clues about what types of furniture and material will inspire him to play creatively.

As soon as children can dress and undress themselves, they love having a closet or wardrobe of their own.

Light-colored walls are soothing to children and help protect their parents' nerves as well!

A dresser can hold all those articles of clothing that don't fit into a closet.

5-Year-Olds

At the age of five, your child's preschool years are drawing to a close. At this stage, girls sometimes seem a bit more mature than boys of the same age. Whereas boys generally prefer to play with other boys, girls may also spend time with adults and with their kindergarten friends of both sexes.

By now your child will have taken over a territory for his play that extends beyond the house or apartment. If you have a yard or garden, your youngsters probably love to run around there for a good part of the day, playing games or climbing trees. Now most children want to play with other children or with adults as often as they possibly can rather than playing alone.

You should get used to the idea that your house or apartment will now become an ever-growing storehouse for all kinds of large, unwieldy playthings: inflatable wading pools, air mattresses, bicycles and tricycles, hopping balls, and roller skates will take up more and more of your space. And then there are the toys that see the most use in winter, when children play indoors: a puppet theater, countless dolls and dollhouses, clothing and accessories, board games, building blocks, cars, etc. You need space for all these things!

If possible, try to set aside an area of your yard or garden where your children can play "outdoors" even in winter without being overly exposed to the weather—for example, a kind of covered winter garden. Many children love spaces like this because they allow them to play outside the home without being too far away from you.

Spending the night with friends also becomes a popular activity at this age, so you may now have the opportunity to welcome young houseguests. Let your child and her friends sleep in a tent the back yard in the summertime. The children will be thrilled by the adventure, and at the same time it will foster their independence. Only you can decide at what age your child is ready for such a venture. Whether she does it at five, six, or seven is not important. Be sure to make it possible for your child to play outdoors with her friends even when the weather is not ideal. It won't hurt her to get a little bit wet! A sandbox is a very popular outdoor play area for preschool children. It doesn't have to be as big as the one at the

playground. Similarly, a swing is a fairly easy thing to set up in your own yard. Does your child like to help out in the garden? Let her have her own little patch of earth where she can plant vegetables or strawberries. This is a playful way to teach a child how to take care of plants. Perhaps you should help her care for them a little bit, since that will significantly increase their lifespan. If you don't have a yard or garden, you can adapt many of these activities to a balcony or terrace. Be creative! It is even possible to purchase a winter garden made of plastic sheeting that will fit onto a city balcony.

Most children are fascinated with nature and feel attracted to everything having to do with the natural world. There are scarcely any children that do not love animals (although they may be afraid of one or two of them), and there is hardly any better playmate for a child than a well-behaved dog. Even a more passive pet, such as a hamster, can be very exciting for a child, and he will enjoy feeding and observing it. Nevertheless, for the animal's sake, it is very

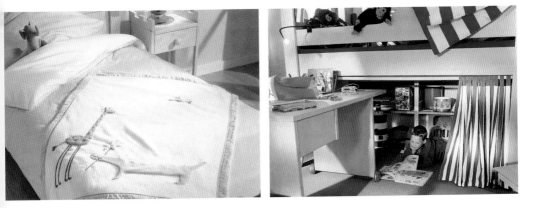

important that such a young child not be given full responsibility for a pet. If you decide to purchase a house pet, you should be absolutely clear about this. Care for the pet together with your child. In this way he can learn to care for it properly, and you can be available to intervene in case a conflict arises between your child and his four-legged friend.

At this age, children are also able to engage in quieter activities, such as reading, for longer periods of time. Does your child enjoy music? Her motor skills should now be developed enough to begin learning a musical instrument. Her verbal skills are gradually becoming fully mature as well. You can now carry on real conversations with your child. Take an active interest in her life. Ask her about her wishes and interests! At the same time, you can also describe your own visions of harmonious family life to your child.

In small children's perception, there is no major difference between a bank building and their kindergarten or daycare center. At best, they

will notice that adults behave differently in different locations. In the first building, grownups carry out serious business and withdraw money for themselves; the second is filled with playing children.

The contrasts between different areas of a home are not as strict, but here, too, children can evaluate the function of any given room based on what they are allowed to do there. The way a piece of furniture looks is not very important to children. The crucial question for them is what am I allowed to do with it or on it? A fancy designer bed frame may look elegant, but if your child doesn't find it comfortable, he won't want to sleep in it for a single night. The lesson for parents is short and sweet: functionality is always the most important criterion.

Light, on the other hand, is far more important to small children than it is to adults. In general, child will find a bright room with large

windows much more pleasant than a dark one with no natural light. Always keep in mind that many children are afraid of the dark. If your child's room contains corners or crannies that don't receive any natural light, you will do him or her a great favor by lighting these areas with lamps.

The quality of the light is also very important—the warmer the better. Cold neon light is more reminiscent of a hospital room than a child's room; would you feel comfortable in such an atmosphere? However, there are energy-saving fluorescent lamps available with special covers that create a warmer light than we typically expect from these bulbs. Unfortunately, they produce a relatively low level of light, and reading with them may be harmful to the eyes (even if your child still reads under the covers with a flashlight, as many of us used to do). Colored light bulbs can create attractive accents and contribute to an inviting atmosphere, but they are not appropriate as an exclusive

source of light. Be sure to provide bright light that extends even to the farthest corners of the room.

And here is one final tip: Preschool-aged children particularly enjoy playing in hallways and entryways. Here they can run barefoot or in their stocking feet—perhaps even play ball—without the danger of breaking something (assuming that your hallway is largely free of furniture). You should therefore decide whether this area of the home should be part of the adult sphere or whether it can be kept free for children as long as they have fun playing there. If you want to allow your children to play here, you will need to first remove any possible obstacles or breakable objects.

Bright light is more important to children than it is to adults. Given a choice, kids will always prefer a bright room with large windows to a dark one with no natural light.

Children enjoy kid-friendly decorations on the walls, and they lend a special atmosphere to a child's room—particularly if you paint them yourself.

Most children can now sleep in full-size bed. At this age they are no longer likely to fall out.

Elementary School Children:
6–9 Years

6-9

Elementary School Children: 6–9 Years

Once your children reach school age, you will not need to change many more things in your house or apartment on their account. It is important that children's beds continue to grow along with them (assuming that they don't already have a full-sized bed). Other than that, you will still be faced with the same mountains of toys—and now there will be books as well. Now is the time when you can unpack your more fragile objects again, since the danger of "earth-quakes" is no longer as great. A school-aged child lives in his own little kingdom quite similarly to the way an adult does. Nevertheless, there are certain points to take into account.

Take special care that your children do not become couch potatoes, particularly if they are already allowed to use a computer. If you have a small terrace or garden, you should definitely allow your child to play there as well. Nowadays, in many schools and after-school care centers, education doesn't only take place inside the building; the learning process is also extended to the world outside. Some teachers take their lessons outdoors in good weather, which children usually love. This is not done with the intention of reviving the liberal educational ideals of the 1970s. Today, teachers simply place more emphasis on learning through direct contact with nature and on

integrating children into their environment. This helps children learn that certain social rules apply not only in the classroom, but in areas of life outside the school as well. For a long time, the indoor and outdoor spheres were strictly divided in pedagogical terms. This led to a situation in which children associated the indoor world with discipline and boring lessons and the outdoors with fun and recreation. Thus, if school lessons move outdoors, meaning that this area is no longer connected solely with fun and play, the converse effect should be that the classroom will not automatically be associated with boredom. In addition, many children are much more relaxed out in the open, since they do not feel as confined. Think back to your own childhood—it is likely that you have more specific memories of events that occurred outdoors.

At elementary school age, children love playing hide-and-seek. Rooms with plenty of recesses and "lairs" are excellently suited to this. Now you will often discover your child hidden under a bed or a table or in

a "hideout" he has built himself. He will almost certainly have gathered the building materials from all over your home. Children's love of small but not too-tight places is quite easy to explain: Children feel most comfortable in spaces that correspond to their own body size. Even if the furniture in their rooms is the right size for them, the height of the ceiling still corresponds to the size of an adult. A little playhouse made of sturdy cardboard will be a source of great enjoyment for your child at this age. It will give him a feeling of safety and security, and besides, inside the house, his own rules of play apply rather than those of his parents.

You should now make it completely clear to your child what kind of behavior is—and is not—appropriate in which areas of the home. As much as possible, you should keep the playing areas of your home open. How many children have access to a 500-square-foot terrace to play on? Be generous and allow your child plenty of room to play indoors. A large dining table is sure to look just as nice next to the

wall as it does in the middle of the room—assuming, of course, that your living area is large enough that you can move the furniture around easily.

The temptation to protect your child from every possible danger that could be lurking in the home is great. It is best to put this thought out of your mind immediately. For one thing, it is nearly impossible; for another, it doesn't make any sense. Excessive safety measures will shield your child not only from every potential danger, but also from every opportunity to learn to do things for herself—a process that can only take place through trying and occasionally failing. The old expression "once bitten, twice shy" still applies today. This may sound a bit harsh, but human nature is programmed to work this way. You can't convince your child of the difference between hot and cold, hard and soft, or dull and sharp by delivering a lecture. She can only learn these things through experience—and yes, sometimes by getting hurt. If you deprive her of the freedom to fail, you will raise a

fragile, unformed person who will tend to give up when faced with the slightest obstacle. Rest assured that your child will not touch a hot stove burner a second time. Children learn quite a bit faster than we do. Don't waste time worrying about unlikely and far-fetched scenarios of danger, and you'll do yourself and your child a great favor.

Elementary school children are continually pushing their physical skills further and further. Their wild jumps and other acrobatic feats often appear quite dangerous to us adults. But in this area as well, children can and should discover the limits of their abilities for themselves. If we don't allow them to test these limits in our presence, they will simply wait until we are not around. Either way, they are sure to do so. Over-anxious concern on our part will have precisely the opposite effect of what we hope to achieve.

At this age, children will also begin to really let loose acoustically and make noise to their hearts' content. They will stretch all of their

abilities—including their five senses—as far as they possibly can. Many children now enjoy making "music" with all different kinds of objects; anything that works well as a percussion instrument is especially popular. For the sake of your own nerves, you might want to limit these activities to specific areas of your home. If your child is seriously interested in music, let him start taking lessons at a music school where he can have the opportunity to learn to play together with other children. For practicing at home, it is best to find a place that is somewhat removed from the rest of the apartment and where the noise will not carry too far outside. Maybe you can remodel a room in your basement for this purpose.

Always keep in mind that games do not simply serve the purpose of passing the time. In the process of playing, your child is also learning about general models of behavior. Consideration for others, as well as the ability to lose at a board game without getting upset, are also skills that need to be practiced.

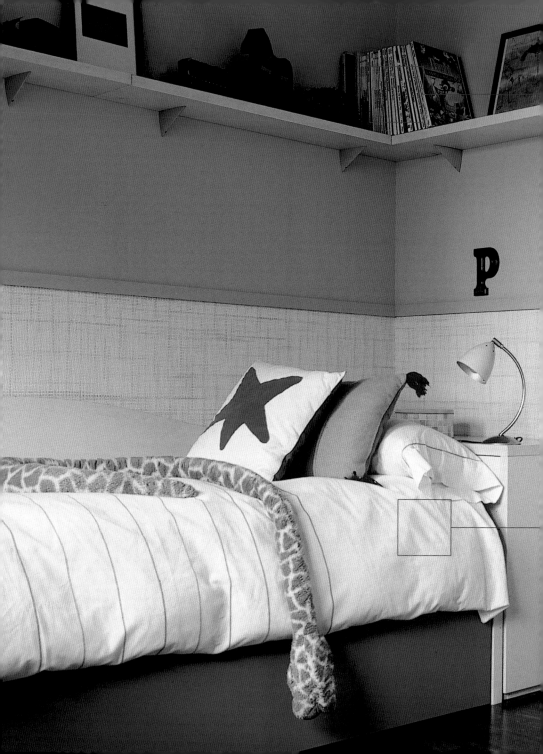

School-aged children should have their own bookshelves where they can keep their treasures.

Any piece of furniture that provides storage space for clothing or toys is a welcome addition to a child's room.

Elementary school children inhabit their rooms in much the same way that adults do. Nevertheless, you should pay attention to certain of their characteristics.

6 and 7-Year-Olds

By age six, most children have discovered television. It is important to establish precise rules from the outset, so that your youngsters don't spend the whole day in front of the TV set. Together with your child, choose one or two appropriate films or series that he is allowed to watch and stay consistent and firm about everything else. Don't make the mistake of "parking" your child in front of the television just because it is so easy to do. For many children, an intense period of manual experimentation is also beginning at this age—a fact that will often manifest itself in paint or pen marks throughout your house or apartment. The best solution is to provide your child with a table at which he can paint or model with clay without being disturbed. Place the table on a floor surface where a few splashes of paint or squashed clay will not be a catastrophe, because these will be unavoidable. At this age, children also begin to practice reading. Your child's activities will thus be a mixture of active games, quieter play such as board games or drawing, and intellectual pursuits such as reading.

At around the age of seven, children first become aware of their limitations as far as physical activity is concerned. For you, first and foremost, this will mean that life will become a little bit calmer, since

you will be able to let your kids play outdoors unsupervised without the fear that they will try to do gymnastics on top of a ten-foot-high wall. Many children this age enjoy taking sports classes or joining an athletic team or club. This provides many advantages for you as well as for your child. Your child will learn specific body coordination together with other children, and she can play and let off steam to her heart's content. When your little athlete comes home, she will probably be so tired in the evening that usual arguments about going to bed are likely to be much less stressful. Furthermore, at this age, your child's sleeping rhythms should gradually be approaching those of an adult.

Naturally, a six-year-old is not yet ready to make all the decisions about the arrangement of his room. He will still need quite a bit of help from you. Nevertheless, you should include your child in the decision process to a much greater degree than you did before—after all, it is his room! Talk with him, ask him about his wishes, and

read between the lines a bit as well. What does your child like to play with most? Does he already exhibit clear preferences? In what room does he spend most of his time?

Does your child like to watch you cook, or perhaps even want to help you? Then set up an area in the kitchen for your future five-star chef where he can play with flour or cut out cookies. Let him wash the vegetables or help you measure ingredients. As a reward, he can serve the food he helped prepare to the whole family. In this way, your child will learn that cooking is not nearly as easy as it looks. It is also an excellent chance for him to learn the names, flavors, and smells of many different fruits, vegetables, and spices. Most children are thrilled to help out in the kitchen.

Don't be afraid to ask your child for her opinion if you are not quite sure what her preferences are. Find out what she does and doesn't like about her room and her play areas. You will be surprised to learn what well-defined opinions school-aged children already have about

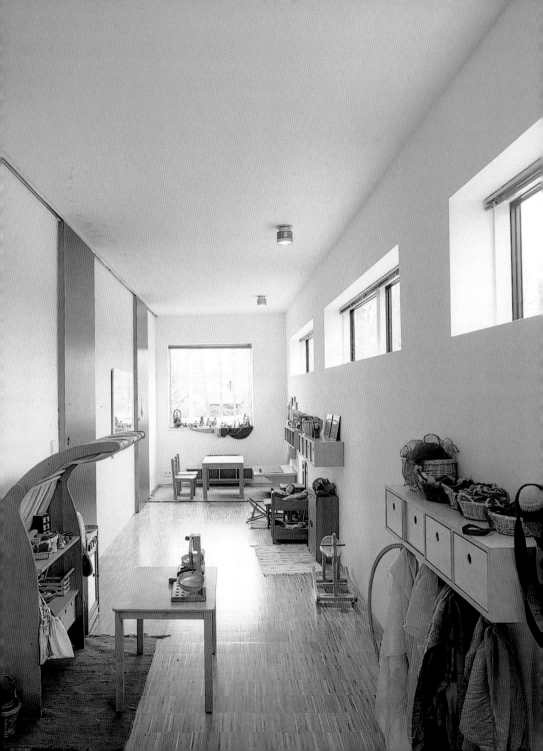

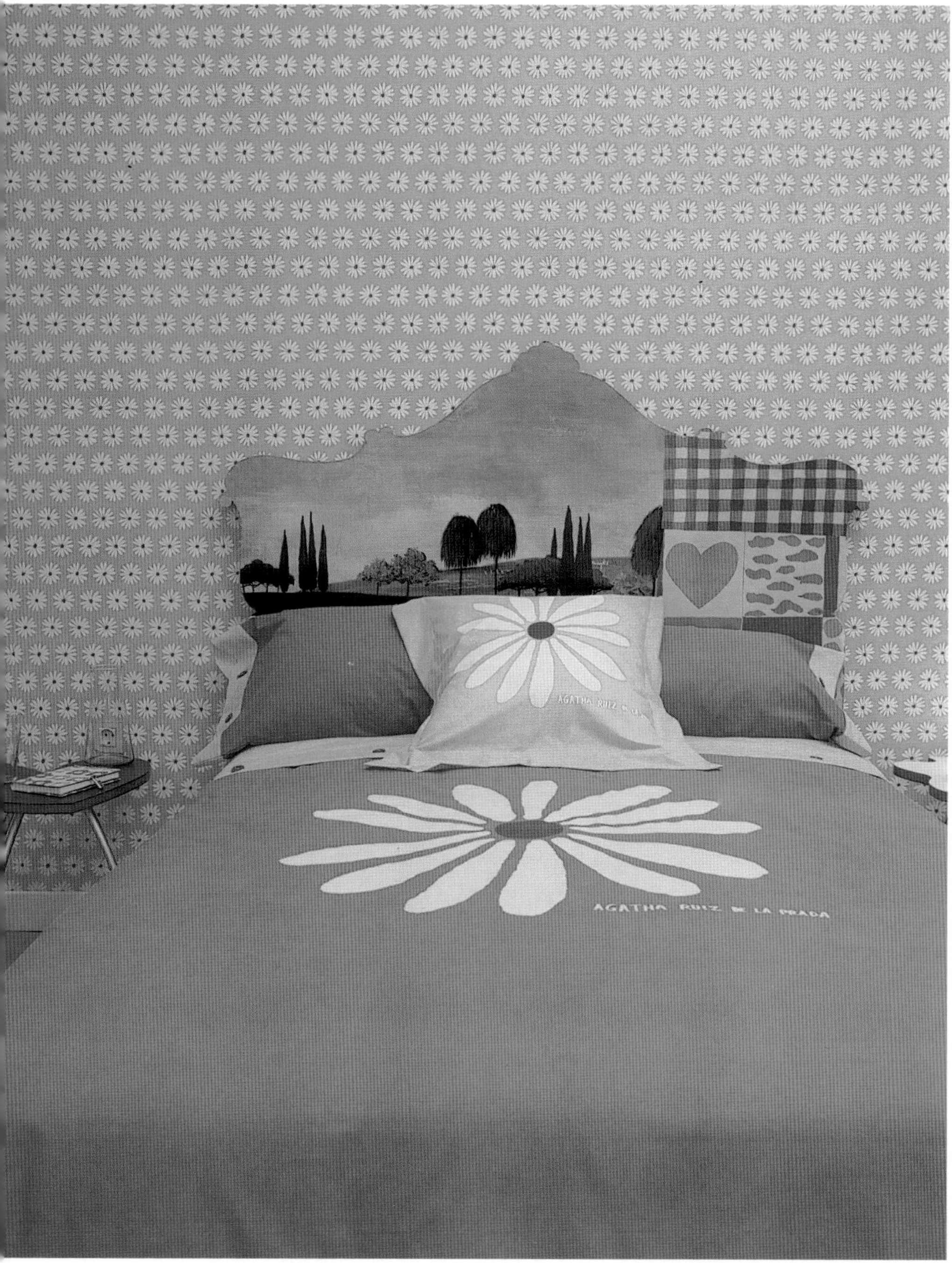
AGATHA RUIZ DE LA PRADA

their needs and wishes, and some of their answers are remarkably mature and logical. The same can be said for the things that they don't like. Now, many children are not only concerned with a given object's functionality, but with its aesthetic appeal as well. Your child will tell you in no uncertain terms whether or not she likes the color of her walls, her furniture, or her bedcovers. Dark colors such as black or gray don't usually appeal to children. Nevertheless, they definitely have their preferences among the lighter and brighter colors. Children often like pastels or metallic tones. However, you should not expect your child to verbally formulate opinions; she might simply say that her dresser is "dumb." Go ahead and ask what she thinks is so dumb about it. Is it the dresser itself? Or perhaps the color? As educators like to say, "Children are experts in everything having to do with themselves."

A playroom in a renovated attic is just the thing for most children.

A desk with drawers provides a surface for writing or drawing. And your child can pretend to "work" just like Mom and Dad.

A stool is a simple, versatile seating option that adapts for all kinds of play.

8 and 9-Year-Olds

Children of eight, nine, or ten have much more in common with twelve-year-olds than they do with six or seven-year-olds. Their personalities are quite well established, and they have developed their own tastes, even if they are still somewhat immature. Now your child will want to have a lot of freedom to decide what his room should look like. With younger siblings, he now plays the role of the strong protector and will sometimes enjoy looking after them. Parents, enjoy the extra freedom this offers you!

By now, your child will have very clear preferences. She may also have begun to display certain special talents. Is she an active, athletic type? Are you raising a young musician—or does she prefer to spend her time reading or drawing? Whatever the case, you should be sure to adapt your child's room and play areas to suit these favorite activities. A bookworm will be thrilled to have a comfortable, well-lit corner for reading, while a talented pianist or a passionate soccer player will be less impressed with such a space. Most likely, your children will have several different hobbies at the same time, which will probably include physical as well as intellectual pursuits. By now, your child will have learned the most important rules of social behavior. For example, an eight-year-old will rarely want to play

soccer in the living room. Slowly but surely, your home will begin to transform itself from a playground back to a place where all members of the family feel equally at home.

School also plays an ever-more-prominent role in children's lives at this age—for example, in the form of homework. Your child now needs a quiet place with his own desk where he can study undisturbed. A dining room or kitchen table is not very suitable for this purpose, since your child will constantly be distracted there. His desk should be large enough, comfortable, and especially well-lit. Ideally, there should be a bookcase within easy reach where he can put away his books and notebooks. Be sure to set aside a special area just for school materials, since they should not get mixed up with your child's toys. Avoid leading him into temptation by removing game consoles and similar items from his study area. At this stage, self-discipline is not yet one of your child's strengths. By the way, did you know that extremely strong exposure to natural light can actually

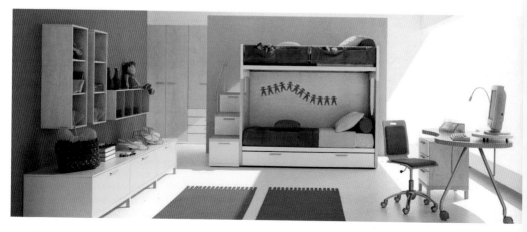

produce slight fatigue? Therefore, it is better to cover your child's windows with blinds or curtains that are somewhat opaque and slightly reduce the influx of daylight. The basic rule for a good learning environment for children is light, yes; sun, no.

By the age of nine, children can concentrate on the same activity for two hours at a time or even longer. In many cases, parents no longer play as major a role in their child's pursuits as they once did. At the same time, you can now expect your child to take part in the routines of the household and to take responsibility for a few day-to-day chores.

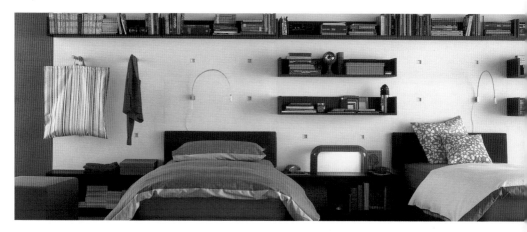

Direct sunlight can have a fatiguing effect, so it is ideal to dampen the light with semi-opaque blinds or curtains.

It is a good idea to separate your child's study area from the play and recreation area by means of a shelf or room divider.

As schoolwork increases, children spend longer periods of time at their desks. Be sure to provide them with a study area that accommodates these higher demands.

Older Children: 10–16 Years

Older Children: 10-16 Years

At the age of about ten, young people begin entering the world of adults. They become aware of their bodies and often more self-conscious. More and more frequently, they retreat into their own rooms and don't want to be disturbed—especially not by uninvited guests. Children's rooms gradually become teenagers' rooms—and of course, they would like this to be evident in the furnishings. But take your time—there is still an enormous difference between an eleven-year-old and a fifteen-year-old. Eleven-year-olds are not nearly as independent as they may sometimes seem to be (or as they would like to be).

Nevertheless, at this stage you should definitely include your child in decision-making that affects the whole family. Choose your vacation destination together, for example. If you are planning to move to a new home, let your child know well ahead of time. After all, she will be greatly affected by it as well. Of course, a child of this age cannot take part in every important decision, but you should still discuss every planned change of environment with her. Simply going over your adolescent child's head to make decisions is asking for trouble. For an elementary school child, it is completely sufficient to take her

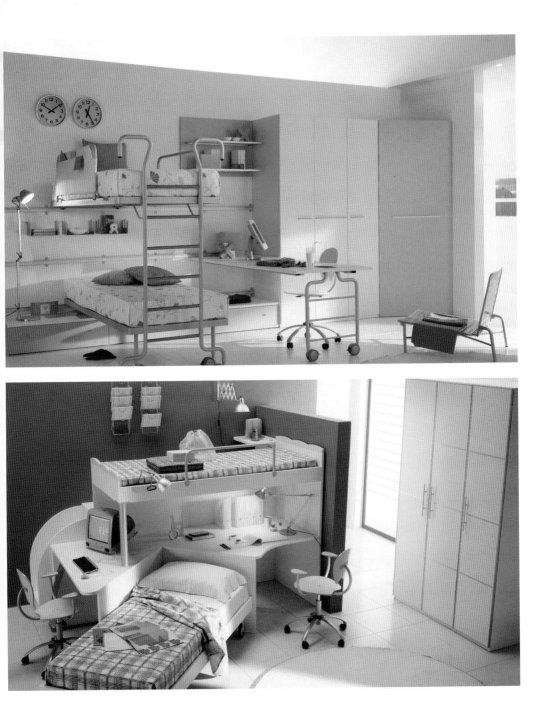

favorite colors into account when designing her room, but starting at around age ten, you should also consult her about her preferences as far as furnishings and their arrangement are concerned. By now, your child will likely have very clear ideas about what she wants.

Outward appearances are now becoming increasingly important to young people. When your child was smaller, it was most important that his room be comfortable and practical; its appearance was usually of secondary importance. This situation will now change drastically. At the age of eleven or twelve, many adolescents begin sacrificing some elements of comfort for the sake of visual appeal. You will notice this first and foremost in your child's clothing style. You should take his choices quite seriously, since this is an opportunity for him to express his personality. Your opinion will no longer play as large a role in the design of your teenager's room. As difficult as it may be, put your own tastes aside and give him the chance to let his imagination go. If he is unsure about the furnishing of his

room, he will turn to you for advice anyway. Try to work together with your child to find a piece of furniture or a decorative element that he likes. This will provide you with a reference point for designing the rest of the room together. A bed is a particularly good object for this purpose, since it is a central element in the room. But you could just as easily choose an attractive lamp or a purely functional item, such as a computer.

Between the ages of twelve and fourteen, most adolescents don't want anything more to do with things that remind them that they were still children up until a short time ago. Now they behave more like adults and remove everything that might seem childish from their rooms—after all, it's not cool anymore. As we all know, the quest for one's own personality is not an easy one, and there will be many false steps and embarrassing moments along the way. Your child's closet should provide plenty of room for "cool clothes," because the older your teenager gets, the more clothing she will

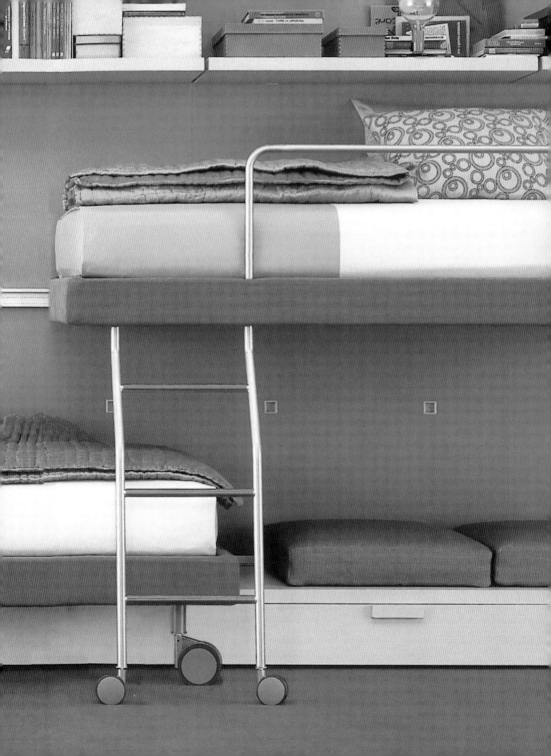

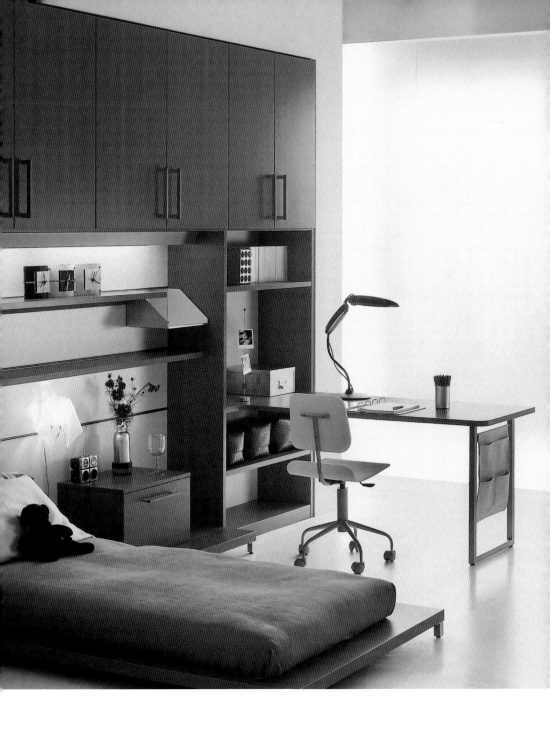

accumulate. Her emerging personality will not only be manifest in her clothing, of course; it will also extend to her taste in furnishings and decoration. Fortunately, it is usually sufficient to simply hang a new poster on the wall rather than replacing all of the furniture every few weeks. This phase in a child's life is not the simplest for any of the people involved. Try to approach it in as relaxed a manner as you can, and remember—even puberty will be over one day.

So now our youngsters' rooms have become a private sphere, where parents are welcome only occasionally. This is where pre-teens and teens listen to music, talk with their friends, play computer games, study for school, or simply relax. The problem at this stage is that almost all the furnishings for a single person's apartment have to fit into one room. Unless you have an enormous home, a well thought-out division of the space is especially important now. Your teenager's room is a bedroom, study, and playroom all in one. The perfect solution for older adolescents might be an accessory apartment

with a separate entrance. In this way, he would not lose his connection to the family, yet he would still have plenty of privacy and independence—and would hopefully learn how to handle it on his own. Unfortunately, very few of us can actually offer our teenagers such a situation.

One good alternative is a so-called modular furniture system, which can be combined in a variety of different ways. This allows you to adapt the furniture in your teenager's room to her varying needs and interests—be she an avid reader or a sports star—and to the situation at hand. If she wants nothing more to do with her children's furniture, she can always pass it on to a younger sibling.

The most important section of a teenager's room is the study area, which needs to satisfy the same requirements as an adult's work area. It is extremely important that the space be very well lit. Ideally, the work place should face a natural light source—that is, a window. Don't be stingy when choosing your child's desk and chair— good

quality is essential here. The chair should be height-adjustable, especially if your child is still growing fast. Some desk chairs have removable armrests that you can attach or leave off according to your teenager's preference. Ergonomically designed chairs force the spine into an S-shaped position, which is easy on the back and allows students to sit for long periods of time. If possible, choose a chair with rollers, which lets you move from the desk to the book-case without having to get up. The desk should be high enough that your child's legs fit comfortably under it. If she uses a computer, the work surface must be large enough to accommodate a monitor, key-board, and mouse pad. In addition, your teenager will need space for school supplies such as notebooks, books, and writing utensils. A good rule of thumb is to choose a work surface with an area four times the total area of all the objects that will be placed on it (that is, computer, telephone, desk lamp, keyboard, printer, books, etc.). If your child's room has an unconventional shape, an L-shaped desk with rounded corners can be a good solution. If nothing else works,

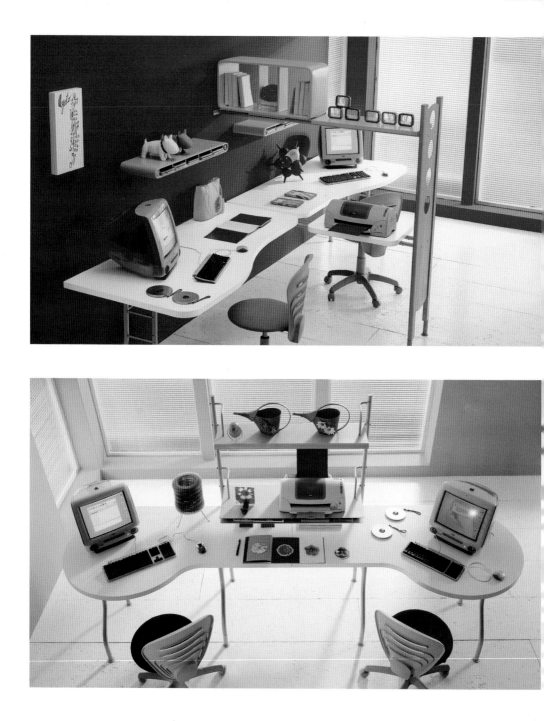

you can have a desktop custom made. This will conserve space by fitting it perfectly into the dimensions of the room, as well as adjusting it ergonomically to fit your child's size. However, since this is a rather costly investment, it is worth undertaking only when your child has stopped growing so rapidly.

You should not immediately rule out any possibility when planning a teenager's room, however unusual it may seem at first. The desk does not necessarily have to stand against a wall or even in front of a large window (although this is advisable). Sometimes your first impulses are the best ones. Move the largest pieces of furniture (seating, tables, bed, and clothes storage) into the room first, then add the smaller ones. Choose the brightest area of the room for the workplace and the darker ones for the bed, dresser, or bookcases. If an area of the room is too dark, be sure to add good lighting. After all, your teenager needs to be able to find his things. A drawer unit is especially practical for storing work materials. The wall that contains

Great Ideas for Children's Rooms

the most electric outlets or a telephone jack is the most logical place for a desk, since it will keep the unattractive but unavoidable tangle of cables to a minimum.

The objects that consume the most storage space in a teenager's room are probably paper of all kinds as well as clothing. Thus, your child should have a separate set of shelves that is sufficiently large for her books, magazines, and the miscellaneous items that boys and girls alike tend to accumulate over the years. This will allow you to reserve the closet or wardrobe just for clothing and frequently-used sports equipment. Today's multimedia computers are making an additional television set or stereo less and less necessary. As a center for all media, the computer is an extraordinarily space-saving element in a young person's room.

The work area is the most important section of a teenager's room. It should be well lit, preferably with natural light. When selecting a desk and chair, quality rather than price should be your first concern.

Teenagers' tastes change constantly—a fact that is not only evident in their clothing. However, it is usually enough to replace the posters hanging over the bed rather than repeatedly exchanging all the furniture in the room.

Even a computer can serve as a decorative element in a teenager's room.

Helpful Hints

Helpful Hints

Many of the observations in this chapter will probably seem quite obvious and logical to you. That makes it all the more astonishing how few parents actually put them into practice in their own homes. And yet they are so simple! With a little imagination, you can turn even the smallest room into a child's dream world.

A. Young children in particular will play with any object they come into contact with, be it a piece of furniture or part of their room's decor. In children's imagination, mirrors, bookcases, kitchen cabinets, curtains, floor lamps, and ironing boards all have lives of their own and are capable of being playmates—even if this is sometimes difficult for us adults to comprehend. Allow your child to have this freedom, and only move the items that could truly be dangerous to a safe place. As much as possible, everything that isn't dangerous should be integrated into your child's room and into his play. (But please don't go so far as to store all the things you don't really want anymore in your child's room!) Before you simply throw away a worn-out pillow, however, you can certainly give it to your child to play with—he will probably be very pleased.

B. Sometimes we fail to take notice of certain differences between our children and ourselves. We have simply gotten used to the way things are in everyday life. However, small children are neither as tall nor as strong as we are. Maybe that is why it is so hard for your child to open and close a solid wood bathroom door. Maybe she can't look out the window because it is simply too high for her to reach without standing on a chair, or she can't reach her favorite picture book because it has been placed too high on a shelf. Fortunately, there are very simple solutions to all of these little hurdles and obstacles—we just have to find them. Did you ever take a conscious look around in your child's classroom or preschool? It's no coincidence that all the chairs and tables are on a miniature scale!

C. Children love their toys. Nevertheless, the mysterious objects that their parents are constantly holding in their hands have a constant, irresistible attraction for little people. This kind of curiosity is completely natural. But be sure to explain to your children that adults'

possessions often break much more easily than their toys made of plastic or wood, and that they must therefore handle them with much greater care.

D. Children love to paint and draw. When it is time to paint a room in your home, let your child help. It is a wonderful experience that neither of you will soon forget. Dress your child in his raincoat, make him a painter's hat out of newspaper, give him a brush, and let him go to it! But do limit his first painting attempts to regular wall paint and plain walls. The acrylic paint used on doors, for example, is very aggressive, and if something goes wrong it is not always easy to correct. When your little helper gets tired of painting, you will still have enough time to adapt his first painting attempts to your desired design and compensate for his mistakes. If your child really likes to paint, you can buy a large roll of paper. Hang it up in a place where a few paint splashes will not be the end of the world, and he can let his creativity run wild. For all painting activities, be sure to provide your artist with appropriate—that is, expendable—clothing.

E. Children's behavior in a room is quite similar to that of cats. They love to hide in inaccessible corners where they think their parents can't see them. They often like to climb up to higher places where they can get a good view of everything going on without being discovered themselves. Children are excellent climbers, and they will try every possible method to get from the bottom to the top of a given object. Nowhere can you see this more clearly than on the ever-popular climbing equipment at the playground and in the acrobatic feats that children perform on them.

F. Children enjoy building and constructing things (and then knocking them over and destroying them)—and they don't limit themselves to wooden or plastic blocks as building materials. They also love discovering larger building elements. Cube-shaped pillows that can be stacked on top of each other are especially popular. Children can integrate almost any object in their environment into their play. Thus, a discarded curtain and a table can become a bedouin's tent, or a

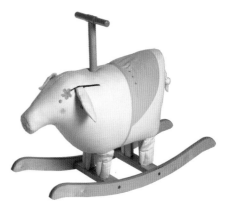

board leaned against the wall can be an enclosure for imaginary cattle. Here, a child's imagination knows no bounds.

G. Even children are often bothered by the noises in our environment. Sometimes they simply want to relax, sleep, or read quietly. Unfortunately, these occasions do not always correspond with their parents' quiet phases. That makes it essential for your child to have a place where she can retreat, where she will not be disturbed by music, the clattering of kitchen utensils, or the vacuum cleaner.

H. Children have a need to try everything out. Most adults, by contrast, prefer to simply read the instructions in order to find out how an appliance works, or read a recipe to help us prepare a meal. Children, on the other hand, need to—and should—try out various possible solutions to a problem in order to decide which one was the best or most successful. They learn instinctively and almost exclusively according to the principle of trial and error, and that is as it should be. Allow your child the time to learn things in this way, even

when it sometimes seems excruciatingly slow and tedious. Just take care that your child does not attempt any dangerous approaches. Our opinions are extremely important to small children, but they are not always capable of translating our words into practice. They believe us, but they don't always understand everything we say. This is why it is so important to let them learn from their own experience—and from their own mistakes—rather than infusing them with wisdom that they believe but don't understand.

I. Many children are enthusiastic chefs. They are thrilled to experiment with you in the kitchen. There are lovely children's play kitchens available with children's dishes to match. Naturally, these plastic dishes are quite a bit more durable than your best china. Nearly every kitchen utensil that is not used specifically for heating food is also available in plastic, and many real ingredients can be found in junior-size packages. Your children are sure to have lots of fun with a

miniature kitchen, and you can count on being invited to sample many of their home-cooked menus.

J. Children like to play in places where they feel protected (from bad weather, for example), but where they still have a good view of what is going on around them. If possible, try to set up a small area in your garden where your children are sheltered from the wind and weather but can nevertheless see out into their rainy surroundings. A winter garden is a good choice for this purpose.

K. "Forbidden" rooms of the house have a nearly magical attraction for children. If you forbid your child to go into certain rooms, you can be assured that he will want to take a look around those very rooms, for that very reason. Is there really any room in your house so dangerous that children should not enter it?

L. Most children are naturally water bugs. Maybe you've been wondering for years whether you should set up a swimming pool in

your backyard. Go ahead! You will make your child the most popular kid in the neighborhood. However, if your child can't swim yet, you must never leave her in the area of the swimming pool unattended. A little slide will also be a huge hit with your child, and all her little friends, too.

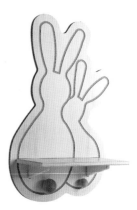

Photo Credits

Photo Credits

Dear (Design) pp. 167, 176

Red Cover/Johnny Bouchie p. 164

Red Cover/Home Base p. 115

José Luis Hausmann pp. 5, 75, 79, 82, 150, 153

Montse Garriga pp. 27, 85, 104, 129, 136, 139

Tisettanta (Design) pp. 158, 169, 172, 181,
190, 234

Ricardo Labougle & Ana Cardinale pp. 99, 173

Leroa (Design) p. 184

J.J. Pérez Iscla pp. 16, 17, 57, 65, 161, 170, 174, 175

Jordi Sarrá pp. 17, 28, 32, 33, 88, 142, 176

Kinderräume (Design) pp. 42, 122

Azcue (Design) pp. 203, 210, 214

Clip p. 45